A Totnes Boyhood

John Legge

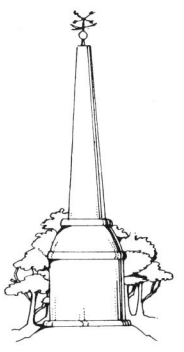

OBELISK PUBLICATIONS

OTHER OBELISK PUBLICATIONS ABOUT THIS AREA

Villages of the South Hams, *John Legge*
The Totnes Collection, *Bill Bennett*
The Great Little Totnes Book, *Chips Barber*
The Ghosts of Totnes, *Bob Mann*
Torquay • Paignton • Brixham, *Chips Barber*
Pictures of Paignton, Parts I, II and III, *Peter Tully*
Brixham of Yesteryear, Parts I, II and III, *Chips Barber*
From Brixham… with love, *Chips Barber*
The Ghosts of Brixham, *Graham Wyley*
Torbay in Colour – Torquay Paignton Brixham, *Chips Barber*
Nine Short Pub Walks in and around Torbay, *Brian Carter*
Torquay United – The First 70 Years, *Laura Joint*
Torquay of Yesteryear, *Leslie Retallick*
Pictorial Torquay, *Leslie Retallick*
Cockington, *Jo Connell* • Colourful Cockington, *Chips Barber*
Dartmouth and Kingswear, *Chips Barber*
The Dart to The Start, *Chips Barber*
Down the Dart – Boat Trip from Totnes to Dartmouth, *Chips Barber*
Dart Country, *Deryck Seymour*
The Ghosts of Berry Pomeroy Castle, *Deryck Seymour*
Film and TV Programmes… Made in Devon, *Chips Barber and David FitzGerald*
The South Hams in Colour, *Chips Barber*
Murders and Mysteries in Devon, *Ann James*
Place-names in Devon, *Chips Barber*
Around the Churches of the South Hams. Parts I and II, *Walter Jacobson*
Walk the South Devon Coast – Dawlish Warren to Dartmouth, *Chips Barber*
Walk the South Hams Coast – Dartmouth to Salcombe, *Chips Barber*
Walk the South Hams Coast – Salcombe to Plymouth, *Chips Barber*
We have over 200 Devon-based titles; for a list of current books please send an SAE to
2 Church Hill, Pinhoe, Exeter, EX4 9ER or telephone 01392 468556

This book is dedicated to my Mother, Father, Sister and the rest of the Family.

Acknowledgements
Especial thanks to the late Bill Bennett MBE, for help with photographs. Also to Anne Santer,
Eileen Iles, Lily Taylor, Bill Santer, Chips Barber and Totnes Museum.

First published in 2005 by
Obelisk Publications, 2 Church Hill, Pinhoe, Exeter, Devon
Designed by Chips and Sally Barber
Printed in Great Britain
by Avocet Press, Cullompton, Devon

A Totnes Boyhood

A Totnes Boyhood

Introduction

Whilst I was growing up in Totnes in the 1950s and 1960s, post-war Britain was starting to push out its 'green shoots' of newly found freedom, and a fresh era was gaining momentum. Traces of another world still remained – cod liver oil and orange juice issues were still obtained at the Ambulance Hall – but a different brush was painting new hues among the fading black and white pictures of a country that still bore traces of the past conflict. Although filled with personal memories, this little book aims to portray what the town of Totnes was like through that time of change. Featured in these pages are many familiar places and faces from that era; some are still around, but, sadly, many have gone.

View from Castle, Totnes.

Welcome to Totnes

Having come from Nelson, Lancashire, in 1937 to live in Totnes, my mother described in her 'memoirs' how Devonshire life was so different from 'the Industrial North' of her youth: "*Totnes had on its best smile to greet me, the Coronation of King George VI and Queen Elizabeth was soon to be celebrated. The main street was lavishly trimmed with red, white and blue garlands, in anticipation of the happy event. What a quaint place it is, next oldest town, (yes! it boasts the distinction of being a town), in England. Narrow streets with an archway over it, once, I suppose, an entrance to the town, it spanned the main street. Quaint Elizabethan houses, with the overhanging storeys typical of that period. Every stick and stone of it breathless Romance with a capital 'R'. Old things and traditions have always intrigued me, they fill me with a sensual delight. Yes I shall love this my future home and feel jealous of the years spent elsewhere.*"

My father, William Legge, had in 1946 arrived home from active service in the Second World War. Two years later he married Doris Chapman, as the picture below shows, and I was born in 1949. We lived in Bridgetown, and I recall that the rented cottage had only a dark cupboard-like place to use as a kitchen; it was probably originally planned as a cupboard for under the stairs. There was no window or sink, and my parents used a marble-topped washstand on which to place a bowl for washing tasks. Somehow they managed to squeeze a gas cooker into this limited space – facilities were exceedingly primitive and cramped in those days!

My early recollections are jumbled rather than sequential: thoughts triggered into motion by events and feelings activated by sights, sounds and smells of long-departed scenes. Totnes has the ability to 'draw' people; my mother had experienced this years before when, one evening, she slipped out to take a look at St Mary's Church. She wrote afterwards: "*It is an impressive edifice,*

and no mistake. Slowly, after leaving the Church, I walked amongst the graves, a few of which were covered with the heavy table-top stones of the 18-century type. Then something unusual happened, at the sight of those old graves, my eyes filled with tears, caused by an emotion I could not exactly analyse. Was it an affinity with those of this area 'gone on' before me. It was almost a sense of being welcomed home amongst them; my ancestors of many generations back had their roots in the West Country."

A Totnes Boyhood

To Smithfields

Mine was a secure, comfortable world within the warmth and protection of family life. At the age of three, however, I entered Torbay Hospital with an inflamed appendix and was operated on just in time, the surgeon removing the offending gangrenous body part. This resulted in a long rehabilitation. Soon afterwards, in June 1952, the family moved from Bridgetown to a housing estate in Smithfields, which looked across to green fields. Below, Copland Lane wound through a lovely rural landscape where cattle grazed and drank from a meandering stream. At intervals the tranquillity would be broken by the roar and hiss of passing steam trains.

In those days there would be just the occasional car parked outside in the road; most families relied on public transport for travel to work or holiday trips.

My mother had a routine, mirrored by most housewives across the country, and would be found on Mondays washing and ironing clothes. The rest of the week was amply filled with even more jobs: the household tasks of baking and cooking; the seemingly endless chores of cleaning the rooms; and sewing and mending garments.

By day, Father worked in Paignton as manager of Devonshire Dairies (previously at Bow's, Co-op and Blackburn's in Totnes). As was usual for men at that time, he would spend spring and summer evenings in the garden tilling the ground, sowing and planting to grow produce to supplement family meals. This was the domestic environment in which I grew up; it is interesting to recall some of the scenes and events that were happening around us in those years.

Coronation Celebrations 1953

On Tuesday 2 June, a cool, wet day, many people lined the streets of the capital on the occasion of the Coronation of Queen Elizabeth II. Those who couldn't be there watched the ceremony on flickering black-and-white television sets. As, at that time, only a small proportion of households owned sets, many who did invited their neighbours to watch this special occasion with them.

Totnes marked the event in grand style. The day's celebrations commenced at 8 a.m., when the parish church bells joyously rang out. This was continued at intervals throughout what proved to be an auspicious day.

Collapark provided the assembly point for a special procession that included the Town Marshal, Fire Brigade, Mace Bearer, Mayor and Mayoress (Mr and Mrs Nott), Deputy Mayor, Kingsbridge Silver Band, clergy and choirs.

These were then followed by schoolchildren from Grove Infants, Church Primary, Redworth Secondary Modern, the High School for Girls and King Edward VI Grammar. It is interesting to recall that in those days there were also four preparatory schools: Bridgetown, Horton, West View and Meadow House.

Behind the assembled schools were Totnes Girl Guides and Brownies, Boy Scouts and Cubs, followed by a loudspeaker van, the Ranger Company, British Red Cross, men's and women's sections of the Royal British Legion, Totnes Lodge RAOB and kindred friendly societies, sporting organisations and supporters' clubs. Finally came yet another loudspeaker van!

At 10.30 a.m. the procession entered Smithfields – the Legge family had a grandstand view! It then made its way along the top Plymouth Road and past Broomborough Hospital. It continued down the High Street, past Fore Street and into Station Road to enter Totnes Borough Park.

Period photographs reveal that the park was very different then; it had a green sward with bandstand and old style cricket pavilion, and there were children's swings, slide and roundabout positioned beside the old rugby and cricket changing rooms.

Steam trains would ply up and down the Quay line beside the park, carrying timber and materials from The Plains. Many a cricket ball ended up in the long grass of the railway embankment, and cricket matches were often held up while white-flannelled figures hunted for them.

A Coronation street party

Here, at the Borough Park, starting at 11 a.m. a United Thanksgiving service was conducted by the Revd Gordon Samuel, Revd F. Ashley and Revd S. W. Townley. This was followed by the broadcast of the crowning ceremony at Westminster Abbey.

A grand Athletic Sports commenced at 2 p.m. There were various age heats: up to age eight years, boys and girls sprinted 50 yards. Medals were awarded along with money prizes of three shillings, two shillings and one shilling for the first three places. The distance increased to 80 yards for the 8–11-year-old age groups; and 100 yards for 11–15 years. In the senior category, the prize money was five shillings for first place.

A Totnes Boyhood

Older children also competed at 220 yards and 440 yards, whilst men's and ladies' races covered 100 yards, 440 yards and 880 yards. There were various obstacle races, slow bicycle competitions, three-legged and sack races for the children. The climax to all this action was a highly competitive tug-of-war contest. Afterwards 'tea' was provided at the Drill Hall for all children over the age of four years. The general public were catered for by a buffet tea at 'popular' prices.

Crowds were entertained by Maypole Dancing, courtesy of Miss Bloomfield, and, at 7.45 p.m., Totnes Castle Grounds provided the perfect setting for *The Queen's Ring*, a one-act play, and for excerpts from *Merrie England*.

After the Queen's Speech at 9 p.m., a procession assembled on Plymouth Road, adjoining Broomborough Hospital. Torches were lit and the brilliantly illuminated procession travelled by way of the town to Bridgetown, Seymour Place, Weston Road and then back over the Bridge to Coronation Road, then to the Borough Park, where a huge bonfire was lit.

At Windmill Down, high above the town, a beacon bonfire was lit, one of a great chain of such fires, which could be seen on prominent hilltop positions across the country.

A grand alfresco dance, between 10.30 p.m. and midnight, was brought to a respectful conclusion by the enthusiastic rendering of 'God Save the Queen'. Thus ended a fully packed day of events for the people of Totnes.

Despite the passing of more than half a century, many people will have their own vivid memories of this momentous day, and it is always interesting to look back at various souvenirs such as photographs and programmes of events. All children under 16 years (before 31 May) were presented with a Coronation mug, plus a box of Widecombe Fair Devonshire toffees, courtesy of the firm Messrs James Marshall (Devon) Ltd. My toffees were soon consumed, but the Coronation mug still remains as a memento of this occasion.

The treats continued the following day. Messrs John Symons and Co supplied a high tea for residents over the age of 65. They were also given the bonus of a free River Dart cruise on Saturday 15 June.

The Grove Infants School

My education began at the age of four. Getting to school was quite an experience. The walk took Mum and me from Smithfields to the top of the town via the higher Plymouth Road. Turning right in the Narrows, we entered South Street with its back entrances, which then included Tarring's Bakery. Here the delicious smell of freshly baked bread wafted in the early morning air. We then passed Wakeham's, a small general store, which, amongst a range of inviting items, sold little packets of sherbet depicting railway engines on the back. Beyond this was the cider depot, on the steep Blueball Hill, where, as children, we could peer through the wooden slats to see crates of dusty bottles. The high walls of South Street, which divide the upper and lower roads, provided another interesting sight along the way, with the ancient rings where horses were once tethered still embedded in the stonework.

The bank opposite the school was a wasteland with struggling elder bushes growing beside little tracks, which were ideal for running and chasing along before school; the elder leaves produced a distinctive smell when grasped.

From time to time a rag and bone man would pass by, much to the delight of the children hanging over the playground wall.

Below the school, but rather overshadowing it, was the gasworks; behind this was a run of houses called Moorashes, accessed by a narrow alley. School dinners were 'enjoyed' at the Mission Hall

in Victoria Street.This building also served other uses, as these two pictures from Christmas 1951 show. The Totnes Mission Hall Club Dinner was a feast to which many looked forward.

The school day began with lining up under the strict gaze of authority before filing into our classes to sit at desk units, these being complete with sunken ceramic inkwells and lifting wooden lids. In the early days of limited equipment, we used slates to write upon before progressing to the more conventional paper and pencil.

Within one classroom was a large picture of the Greek legend of Persephone. It showed a young woman standing in a field of flowers whilst impending doom was about to overtake her in the form of a chariot driven by Hades bound for the Underworld. This darker side must have influenced my artistic efforts, for black was the most prominent colour in any paintings produced!

A Totnes Boyhood

Classrooms too tended to be painted in sombre colours, and there was little in the way of the visual aids or classroom displays that exist today. It is now the Grove County Primary School. Founded in 1865, it reflected the sturdy but uninspiring design of Victorian times. Also, being in a large class meant less attention was given to individuals and group teaching was not an integral part of the curriculum; lessons were taught to the whole class with virtually no allowance for those who struggled to grasp the basics. Thus such an event as a Nature Walk was something to be treasured; I remember we escaped into the outside world for a morning once, taking the route along a little lane behind the school, where we encountered an environment of hedges, trees and fields. I believe it could have been the fascinating track called Fishcheaters (Fishchowters) Lane; some 30 years later I walked the same track with my mother, noting how small it looked.

My sister Anne was born when I was six years old, but at the time I was languishing in bed with a bout of measles. Other common ailments of that era included mumps, chickenpox and whooping cough. At least the time off school when sick gave some relief from the monotony of a daily educational diet of 'Janet and John' stories, 'Old Lob', spellings and times tables.

The Market Hall

Built in 1848, Totnes Market Hall was always an interesting place to walk around. There was a fascinating second-hand bookstall; amongst the books on one occasion they had a huge copy of John Bunyan's works including *Pilgrim's Progress*. There was also a stall kept by Mrs Hopkins, from Paignton, who sold home-made boiled sweets. In the entrance was a lady who sold second-hand goods including musical instruments, which she would demonstrate by playing them.

It was at the Market Hall that children had celebrated VE Day by dressing in a variety of costumes. This photograph shows the outside of the building. Amongst my 1950s memories is the disastrous fire that totally destroyed it. As the conflagration raged, the billowing smoke could be seen from our upstairs bedroom window.

On 11 May 1960 Totnes people were able to witness the opening of their new Civic Hall, a building that came up to everyone's expectations. It was described by one authority as *"Hung with its heavy coat of grey slates, windowless on the world that passes up and down the main street, and mounted on tall concrete columns – that's the new Totnes Civic Hall! Stairs swing up airily like the flying buttresses of a medieval cathedral on one side of the grey façade and, on the other, the approach is by a long smooth ramp. Inside, with a wide stage and seating for 334 people, there is future promise of plays, conferences and exhibitions."*

Totnes had become well-known for theatrical productions such as *Pirates of Penzance*, which was staged in 1950. That same year St Mary's Parish Church presented their Christmas pageant, *Light is Come*.

Now there was a brand new venue to provide a home for plays. This photograph shows one of them – *Trial by Jury*, which was performed by the Totnes Amateur Operatic Dramatic Society in 1965.

I am indebted to the late Bill Bennett MBE, who sadly passed away in October 2004, for letting me use these pictures. He was a wonderful man who served the town so long and so well that his nickname of 'Mr Totnes' was richly deserved.

Totnes Church School

In 1957, at the age of eight years, I walked a new route to my new school. This time the way led through the town and under the ancient Butterwalk. We would often make the brief diversion into Manning's (later Morris's) sweet shop; here there were such delicacies as pink candy prawns and sherbet flying saucers.

In those days, W.H. Smith was just above Woolworths. A copy of the *Eagle* (a children's comic published from April 1950 onwards) could be purchased for a mere threepence; during wet playtimes further copies could be read in the classroom, where there was a supply of other amusing comics such as the *Beano* and *Dandy*.

Another interesting little shop selling sweets, across from the Butterwalk, was Fordham's.

The dreaded dentists' surgery was placed just before Church Close; here, from time to time, we would have to endure fillings and extractions. In some cases a trip to Totnes Cottage Hospital was required to have more difficult extractions by means of the dreaded 'mask'. On such awful occasions ether was administered.

Turning into Church Close, feet would clatter on the uneven cobbled surface of a path overshadowed by the towering edifice of St Mary's Church. At about 8.40 a.m., juvenile figures would make their way towards one of two entrances to Totnes Church School: the Boys' entrance was in Church Close, whilst the Girls' gate was at the North Street end. Some children travelled from as far as the outer reaches of Westonfields and Pathfields in Bridgetown, whilst the remainder hailed from all the other parts of Totnes. On arrival they all congregated in the school playground.

There would always be a smattering of parents bidding farewell to their offspring. The early arrivals often sat on the churchyard wall whilst waiting for school to commence. The last ones to arrive, sometimes half-dressed and finishing the remnants of a hurried breakfast, were usually the children living nearest to the school!

Activities inside the playground included swapping matchbox labels (of which there were countless examples in an era when smoking was a common occupation) and the latest Brooke Bond tea cards (consisting of various different collectable series of bird portraits, British wildlife, wild flowers and freshwater fish). Each packet of tea contained a colour picture card with an image on one side and information relating to it on the reverse. Albums could be bought to stick them into.

On the playground wall there was a cylindrical object. This was a siren that had been used to good effect in the Second World War. My Aunty Vera attended Church School at that time and remembered being in an upstairs classroom when, on looking out of the window, the children spotted a low-flying plane level with the school. The siren sounded and 'Fatty' Williams, their teacher, ordered the children to exit the classroom. However, as they congregated on the landing there was a huge blast, which sent the whole class crashing from the top to the bottom of the stairs. As they landed in a jumbled heap on the ground floor, a final crash announced that the teacher had also arrived – with the blackboard on top of him! The bomb fell on Priory Avenue, taking out a complete house. Aunty ran all the way to Bridgetown, reaching home safely.

Another incident concerned a boy who fell from the top floor, only to be caught by his braces on a coat-peg below. Despite having to be rescued, rather like a dangling parachutist, he escaped unscathed!

Entering the Church School in 1957, we embarked upon a programme of learning that was subdivided into basic skills (reading, handwriting and arithmetic), English (language, speech, written English, use of library and spelling), environmental work (geography, history, nature and practical mathematics) and creative work (art, craft, needlecraft and hygiene – "Hi Genie", as we called it). The curriculum also embraced religious knowledge, physical education and music.

Our classroom in Class One (we were graded 'A' stream for odd numbers, 'B' stream for

even numbers) was situated beside the boys' playground, with two windows facing in that direction. The Headmaster, Mr Bennett, had his office on one side as we turned through to a room that had serried ranks of desks facing the teacher's desk. We sat with our backs towards the window.

Each desk had a lifting lid, heavily personalised by previous incumbents. The inkwells were invariably clogged with remnants of blotting paper. These could be speared with a pen nib during dull periods when lessons dragged. When used properly, these inkwells were filled by a container with a long thin spout rather like a deformed teapot!

The teachers of that era included Miss Hayward,

Mr Bryant and Mr Taylor, who achieved some excellent results with recorders and music. Some years later, when I entered the teaching profession, I took on his class and had the strange experience of sitting in his teacher's chair. The real bonus was that I then faced the window! Teachers in charge of other classes from 1957 to 1960 included Mr Smith and Miss Hill. When Mum had taken me, and later Anne, to school, she enjoyed staying and watching from outside the gate as Miss Hayward took her PE classes in the playground, marvelling at her complete control of the 'masses'.

Assembly was held in the main hall. A copy of the famous painting *The Laughing Cavalier*, who appeared to smile benignly upon countless generations of pupils, was positioned in a high place overlooking the room. This was at the far end, where a flight of steps led to the first-floor classrooms. The school kitchens, where my Aunty Mavis worked at one time, were to one side of the stairs. However, several of us forwent the delights of school dinners and ate at home, as there was sufficient time for the two-way journey.

My first school report showed an inclination towards English (I found mathematics a pointless chore). In my Class Three end of term report I finished 14th out of 38 pupils with the comment "Works well in short spasms, wants to stop and play."

One of the most interesting lessons was craft, taken by Mr Howard, for which the boys focused upon the construction of a model yacht. However, I'm not sure mine ever reached the maiden voyage stage!

The playground was small, and PE involved setting out rush mats on which various gymnastic feats were attempted. Games sessions were held at the Borough Park with the occasional game of football, reminiscent of a flock of sheep huddling around the ball. On wet games afternoons we would sometimes have an art session, or it would be 'business as usual' with curriculum tasks.

Sports Days were also held in the Borough Park and included such enterprising team games as 'putting the ball in the hoop' and 'Corner Spry'. My diary for 1959 records that Reds beat Blues by 126 to 119 points.

Being a Church school we had close ties with St Mary's Church, so Harvest Festival, Ascension Day, Christmas and Easter were tied in with appropriate services.

In addition to these religious times, a Leavers' Service was held at the end of summer term. 'God be with you till we meet again' was sung with feeling.

The final year at Church School was spent across the path from the old building in one of the wooden huts, where Class Seven was based. At this time one of the highlights was the annual Christmas trip to Dartington Hall, where the school was entertained in the theatre with a play called *The Three Kings*.

Occasionally, we were required to put on a show of country dancing, but, as there were more boys than girls, we boys often partnered one another, which led to a good deal of horseplay! One year the event was filmed for television.

Another highlight was the visit to the Romany Cinema, when all the school was escorted the short distance up the street, past Woolworths, and into the 'pictures'. We were treated to a cowboy 'cliffhanger' followed by *Scott of the Antarctic*, starring John Mills as Captain Scott. On another occasion we watched *Under the Sea* (1954), a natural history film. Such pleasant diversions proved to be a most welcome change from lessons.

Managing to fail the national eleven-plus examination, I was now ready to join those destined for Redworth County Secondary Modern School. It was the parting of the ways, as some of my friends were to go to the Boys' Grammar School or the Girls' High School.

Anne started Church School when I left; this 1960s class photograph is taken in the old boys' playground. In later years, the school even boasted a swimming pool, but the school is no longer in existence. Today, Totnes children attend either the Grove County Primary or St John's Church of England Primary, Bridgetown.

Before the old site of the Church School was redeveloped, I took some interesting snaps of the locations. It revived the smells of chalk dust and stale milk that had pervaded our senses all those years earlier.

'Lighten our Darkness'

In the early 1950s, when we first moved out to Smithfields, our lighting and heating relied upon gas for power and energy. In the council houses we had the old gas mantle, which Dad would light each evening. The rooms would be lit with a dull glow. It was wonderful when, a few years later, electricity brought added brightness to our modern homes.

Outside the house, in the middle of the triangle, was a street lamp, with bars below the lighted lantern where a ladder could be propped for maintenance. This was the focal point for the local children, particularly at night and in the dark winter evenings. Amazing gymnastic stunts would be performed using the bars; it was common to see someone perched on top of the lamp itself!

Leisure Time

It is always interesting to look back on those precious 'out of school' times, be it holiday, or just the evenings and weekends.

The annual autumnal game of conkers came into its own when the horse chestnut trees, such as those on the Island, in nearby fields, or the one opposite the Doctor's surgery, bore their fun-filled fruit; these would be raided and left bare.

Chestnut Tree, Tot

Next came the excitement of Bonfire Night and firework displays. Weeks before the big night, groups of children would travel around the estate asking for any contributions to the bonfire. This was built in a little field behind the houses. On the night, the smoke and flames could be seen from all around. Hours of preparation went into the most elaborate Guys, only for them to be extinguished in the flames.

It was also the custom for every household to put on its own modest firework display. Anne and I would wait with great excitement for Dad to arrive home from work; as it grew dark, the whole neighbourhood would echo to the various sounds of Catherine Wheels, Traffic Lights, Rockets and Bangers.

There was always a danger element; one of my friends, who lived a few doors below, had some fireworks in his pocket and a stray spark ignited them, causing a lasting scar.

I used to collect plastic kits of railway engines and took great pleasure in popping a banger in the boiler of a steam train to re-create, in miniature, a scene similar to that seen in the film *The Bridge on the River Kwai*.

We collected and swapped plastic kits such as Airfix, which launched in 1952 with a model of *The Golden Hind* followed the next year with the Spitfire. And there was my favourite, Kitmaster, which produced some magical train kits: Blue Pullmans, Battle of Britain, Duchess of Gloucester, Deltics, Prairie Tanks and so on.

Christmas 1959 saw me receiving two 'Harrow' class engines, as Uncle Eric and Aunty Mavis had the same idea as Mum and Dad, but I was thoroughly satisfied. Cumming's Toy Shop and Mrs Seymour's corner shop in The Narrows were dealers. They also sold Keil Kraft balsa wooden aeroplane kits, which required massive patience and skill. Before any assembly could be attempted, one had first to cut out all the parts with a razor blade before placing and sticking on a wax plan. The framework was then carefully covered with tissue paper before painting over with 'dope', which stretched and hardened the covering. Incidentally, you could get really 'high' whilst doing this! After sticking the fuselage, wings, tailplane and fin in position, the plane was painted. Groups of us would assemble for the 'take-off', powered by a delicate elastic mechanism and usually over

the fields. Needless to say, many hours of painstaking work often ended in a tangled mass of wreckage just a few feet away. Sometimes they didn't get even that far…

Having completed the most perfect model of my fleet, I laid it on the bed to dry. It being a dark, cold winter's night I had a hot-water bottle – the ancient stone type, which was very heavy. At bedtime, before switching on the light, I placed it on the bed – with the inevitable, heart-rending, model-breaking result!

As car ownership was not the norm, there were few cars either travelling or parked in our road, so groups of children playing football or cricket in the street were a common sight, particularly when it was too wet to go to the park or into the fields.

Sometimes we would play 'tracking'. A pair would run away, being given a fair start, and the rest of us would hunt these 'fugitives' down.

Prior to the Totnes–Kingsbridge by-pass being built, we had the isolated bridge (now passing over the road from Lower Collapark) as a place to scale. Another good place to play was the drainage pipe, which was usually quite dry and led under the main railway line below the railway bridge.

Before the alteration of the road system on this side of town, the original main road ran steeply down to Malt Mill and then climbed Castle Hill. My memory of travelling this route by bus makes me wonder how such narrow roadways coped, even then. Until recently it was possible to see a section of the old road embedded in the grassy bank.

Our best playground was the fields at the bottom of the Smithfields estate. To reach this haven required commando-style tactics, for it lay beyond Totnes Cemetery and the railway line. Firstly, a fence partitioning the small field from the cemetery had to be negotiated. Far more difficult was the avoidance of a wonderful elderly lady called Bertha Winchester. She was the gravedigger, and

guarded her territory well; she was always on the look-out for any trespassing juveniles. Upon reflection, she did a marvellous job and kept the cemetery in pristine condition.

The next obstacle was the stream under the railway bridge; with the aid of wellington boots, the track across the marsh would be gained. A barbed-wire fence blocked the exit, so had to be crawled through. A final leap over another small stream, and freedom was gained!

To the left was Sherwood Forest, which frequently resounded to the sounds of Robin Hood's outlaws being tracked by the Sheriff's men. Sherwood Forest was a small tract of woodland with beech trees frequented by nuthatches. It had deep undergrowth, ideal for evading the enemy.

In order to proceed further, a log across a stream needed to be carefully negotiated. On the far side of the wood, open fields rose steeply to a small quarry where milk churns from Dawe's Creamery had been discarded. These were man-handled (or child-handled) to the top of the hill. This achieved, they were then set rolling back down the hill with ever increasing speeds. The railway line was at the bottom, but I cannot recall a churn breaching the fence!

Upstream from the wood was marshy ground, which extended as far as Whiteley Bridge. It was an alternative amusement to wade along the shallow stream, where bullheads (or miller's thumbs) could be caught. On hot summer afternoons cattle would wander down from the water meadows to drink in the stream, where low branches of hazel overhung the water in places. Water-rats betrayed their presence by a sudden splash. Stickleback and, occasionally, small rainbow trout frequented these spots of tranquillity.

Sometimes, the peace would be shattered by the clatter and roar of freight trains pulled by a 28XX, or perhaps by the celebrated Cornish Riviera express as it tore through the Totnes countryside. Detonators, used on the line as a warning, were stored in a gangers' hut near our wood. On one occasion, its door was found open by a group of children – and the contents provided another noisy distraction.

During the Second World War a goods truck carrying cauliflowers was derailed on this stretch of line. Local inhabitants were able to supplement their diet!

Our rough and ready cricket pitch was set on a small level plateau amidst hilly fields. Here, the local lads would play the game whilst imagining themselves as their cricketing heroes: Peter May, Colin Cowdrey, Frank 'Typhoon' Tyson, 'Fiery' Fred Trueman or 'Lord' Ted Dexter. Perhaps these flights of fancy could be attributed to the bubblegum cards, which were so enthusiastically collected. These bore portraits of the stars and career statistics. A schoolboy's imagination would transport our rural pitch to the crowded scenes of Lord's or the Oval.

Incidentally, many years later Charlie Griffiths, the great West Indies fast bowler of the 1960s, came to play in a cricket match on the Borough Park at Totnes, and I have this photograph of him standing beside the pavilion.

An interest in wild flowers led me, Anne and friends through the fields and lanes looking for and identifying common types such as snowdrop, primrose, bluebell, wild rose and foxglove, but we also discovered rarer species such as the beautiful, fragrant lesser butterfly orchid. In later life, this knowledge of the countryside proved most useful in job interviews.

At this time, a common practice was collecting birds' eggs, which, quite rightly, is now a forbidden practice. Once, I scaled a tall pine at Follaton to examine some jackdaws' nests, much to the annoyance of the birds and also the local inhabitants. On the way down, however, I fell from quite a height and, trying to catch hold of a passing branch, missed and badly scratched my leg. The mark has remained, and the jackdaws still nest beside the Council offices.

A Royal Visit

In July 1962, Queen Elizabeth II visited Totnes to open the new cattle market. This replaced the Rotherfold site, which is shown here. Despite boasting such obvious advantages as railway sidings, rings, pens, offices and car parking, it ultimately proved to be a bad move, and the new out-of-town venue, on the site of the old racecourse, became a 'white elephant'. Although it proved to be a

commercial failure, local children found the cattle areas very convenient for cricket and football. It was also ideal for driving lessons, and was well used by instructors to get pupils familiar with controlling a car! Today it is the site of the town's industrial estate.

A victim of its own success, the original market, at the top of the old town, could not cope with the amount of trade being passed its way; the new market had been seen as the perfect solution.

Crowds gathered to see Her Majesty pass by. A small group of us found a suitable watching post along Station Road. Meanwhile, my mother and Anne were invited to watch at Mrs Stoyle's house situated at the beginning of Plymouth Road (as seen in the picture).

Totnes Walks

Apart from the occasional taxi, most families relied upon public transport for getting about. This also meant that going for a family walk was a much more common activity, and Totnes was well placed for a number of excellent country rambles. One of our regular routes took us up Kingsbridge Hill to a point beyond the Toll House. We would then turn off onto Windmill Down and travel along towards Jackman's Lane, passing the reservoir. We completed the 'circular' journey by way of Follaton.

Occasionally, we ventured across the fields to the picturesque village of Ashprington, where my father was born (see another of my books, *Villages of the South Hams*, which also features Tuckenhay, Cornworthy, Harbertonford and East Allington).

There were some lovely walks along the River Dart using the footpath that led beside the weir and on to Dartington Woods. This formed part of the Redworth Secondary Modern cross-country running course.

We explored in many directions. Sometimes we would walk to Windwhistle Cottage, high above the Dart, or along the Newton Road to the caves where tramps would reside.

Another route took us up Barracks Hill, so called because it was the site of the 19th-century Totnes Barracks. Only the cellar remains. It is strange to believe that along the quiet Longcause, soldiers prepared for the invasion of Napoleon's army. On one tragic occasion, a group of soldiers took out a leaky old boat onto the River Dart near Dartington, and all of them drowned.

Coplin Lane, now known as Copland, was a lovely leafy alternative route to Barracks Hill. When travelling further afield, public transport was often a necessity: major shopping trips, days out, medical appointments and work-related duties usually required such services.

For essential trips, a taxi was used. On Christmas Day 1959, when Mum was convalescing at Moretonhampstead's Cottage Hospital and there was no other way of getting to see her, Mr Jordan drove us through the pouring rain to this moorland town. As the driving rain fell across the valley we were able to look down on the old branch line from Newton Abbot to this remote destination, where 45XX tank locos would puff along the winding track.

On the Buses

Bus journeys invariably started or finished on The Plains, where there was once a Western National booking office. The bus depot, where vehicle cleaning and general maintenance took place, was located in nearby Ticklemore Street, .

A red-liveried Devon General bus would be taken if we went to visit Aunty Vera and Uncle Cyril at Uphempston. She worked at Bray's, the chemist shop in the Narrows. On her half-day off, Mum, Anne and I would meet her at Bray's and then walk down to The Plains, where we would take the bus to Shadrack Cross, then walk down the hill to the hamlet of Uphempston. Our return journey was often by courtesy of Uncle Cyril, who would kindly

give us a lift home in his Morris 1000.

My father used to catch the Western National bus for his daily journey to work in Paignton. The alternative, less direct bus route was the hilly, but picturesque, journey through Berry Pomeroy, past Barton Pines and then down the very long, red sandstone hill to Collaton St Mary on the main Paignton road.

In 1967, my first teaching assignment was at Curledge Street School in Paignton, so this also became a familiar bus journey to me.

When travelling in the Plymouth direction, the bus would call at locations such as Ugborough, where the Church of St Peter, overlooking the village square, made an impressive landmark.

Summer holidays would sometimes include a bus ride to Holne. We had to travel on a Wednesday as this was the only service of the week from Totnes; the vehicle would slowly wend its way along the winding narrow roads, the gears grinding as the driver negotiated the steep inclines. On arrival our family would alight in this picturesque village, then, laden with a picnic meal, we would make the uphill walk to the edge of the open moorland of Dartmoor. The alfresco meal was all the more enjoyable for the effort put in to reach the superb Holne Moor.

Benefiting from a bus depot of its own, Totnes was also the starting point for a range of coach trips, day and half-day, to such locations as the Doone Valley, Tintagel, Boscastle, Looe and Polperro, Fingle Bridge, Newquay and Becky Falls; there was also the inevitable Mystery Tour. I recall that all of them seemed to provide excellent value for money.

There were also coach tours for groups, such as the retirement pensioners seen here in June 1956.

Local Railways

In the age of steam, the most exciting travel moments usually came on railway journeys; to travel behind those steam-hissing, smoke-belching monsters was a memorable experience.

My first memories of the railway in Totnes date back to the early 1950s, when my father would take me in a pram to the station, on a Sunday afternoon, usually to coincide with the arrival of the 3.15 p.m. from Plymouth. On one occasion an experimental gas turbine locomotive trundled through Totnes – but I never saw it again.

A Totnes Boyhood

In those days Totnes station was much more of a busy community, employing many workers. It was the start point for railway pilgrimages to faraway places (at one time you could catch a train direct to Inverness) and was depicted colourfully on railway posters. From the old Great Western Railway footbridge, dating back to 1888 (and sadly destroyed by a crane!), it was possible to watch expresses thundering through, or, much more sedately, cattle wagons unloading stock. Another common sight at Totnes were the milk trucks. These were joined by a hose to the milk lorries of the creamery. The early-morning smells of Dawe's Creamery, situated beside the station, wafted the distinct scent of dried milk on the air to be mingled with the aroma of fried breakfasts from the porters' room.

A water tower stood at one end of the station for many years, but it eventually succumbed to the ravages of nature. Even its remains have been demolished and removed.

The walk from home to the railway station was always one full of anticipation and, sometimes, even apprehension, as we hurried to the booking office with the sound of a distant whistle from County, Hall or Castle Class locomotives appearing around the bend.

There were other activities usually going on. The engine shed and goods shed, at the end of the platform, were a hive of activity with busy Prairie tank-engines running around on shunting and banking duties.

The steep inclines of Dainton, near Newton Abbot, and Rattery, on the climb to the edge of Dartmoor, made life hard for the trains of those times.

Staverton Station in more recent times

Some locomotives had an easier life. Bulliver, the 14XX class engine, shuttled a flatter route between Totnes and Ashburton, calling at country stations such as Staverton and Buckfastleigh. But this branch wasn't to survive the cut-backs. Shortly after the line closed, a group of us walked along the derelict tracks then devoid of railway life. It was amazing to see how soon nature encroached on the railway.

In its working life, the Ashburton branch provided some wonderful childhood memories for me. I clearly recall mother regularly taking us by train to the pretty station of Staverton; having alighted, we would walk down a track, over the rails and spend a sunny afternoon in the shallow waters of the Dart looking for fish, before having a picnic tea.

My cousin, Jim, gave me a book called *The Observer's Book of Steam Locomotives*, and, along with many trainspotting mates, I also eagerly collected train numbers. We would pester the drivers and firemen of 'Bankers' to let us join them on the footplate. Sometimes regulations were waived and the delights of the cab were enjoyed. On one occasion we were invited to join in a meal of curried beans, cooked in the boiler, but politely refused.

There were repeated journeys to Newton Abbot, a very busy rail centre, sometimes to visit some of Dad's relations, Aunty Minnie and Uncle Ned. At other times, along with school friends, we went there in pursuit of our hobby. This occasionally involved the sort of tactics that mirrored those

employed in *The Colditz Story* (1954), a film which was familiar to cinema goers at that time. To the south side of the station were the locomotive shed and works, and the outer part of the railway yard; to access the wonders available in this forbidden area meant evading sentries and involved a certain amount of climbing. We were well rewarded for our 'gung-ho' efforts because we eventually came away with a crop of train numbers for the collection. However, as we moved into the 1960s, steam trains were phased out to be replaced by diesel engines.

Exeter St Davids railway station was another holiday venue where the joys of Southern Region engines could be seen. In the opposite direction lay Plymouth and its Navy Days, the

Hoe and its big, modern stores. Mum also took us by rail to Brixham, where her friend Hazel lived. The little branch line from Churston ended high above the fishing town. Like so many others, it is now long gone.

The 'Beeching Axe' deprived us of repeating many favourite rural train rides. In particular I remember the sheer loveliness of the branch line that ran from Brent down the Avon valley to Kingsbridge. En route the train passed through gorgeous scenery and some de-

lightful little stations, such as Avonwick, Gara Bridge and Loddiswell. Known as the Primrose Line, it lingers long and pleasantly in the memory.

The Dart

Now referred to as Vire Island, to honour our twin town, The Island was a favourite location, with its ample space to play hide and seek amongst the bushes, collect conkers or feed the swans and ducks. We would sometimes watch the timber for Reeves being unloaded from Scandinavian or Russian vessels. We would also delight in seeing the paddle steamers churning through the waters of the Dart. These wonderful vessels had such names as *Compton Castle*, *Kingswear Castle* and *Totnes Castle* and would ply up and down between Totnes and Dartmouth, but, having given long years of faithful service, were becoming somewhat 'worn out'.

One of the 'sights' of the river trip was the sewage works, built in 1907 and located near World's End. At one time there were cottages at World's End; one can only imagine what life was like in this remote spot. Similarly 'in the wilds' on the left bank is Windwhistle, the ruins of a farm cottage last inhabited in the early 1900s. Journeys by paddle steamer would be accompanied by commentary; such interesting (but inaccurate) facts as Sharpham House being a calendar house with a supposed 365 windows and 52 rooms would be relayed to impressed passengers as they looked up to this amazing structure!

The trip to Dartmouth is certainly an uplifting and refreshing experience, and one we enjoyed from time to time.

Another water-based 'amusement' was the annual Totnes Regatta; it was possible to hear the loudspeaker from the immense heights of Totnes Down Hill when the results of the rowing events were announced.

Redworth County Secondary Modern School

A long concrete drive, bordered by grass-covered pavements provided the entrance to the former Redworth Secondary School. Stretching away on either side, beyond the fenced pathways, were verdant playing fields; on the left pitches rose upwards to farming and gardening areas, whilst to the right more playing areas were bordered by fir trees marking the course of the Ashburton Road. As they topped the rise, pupils, resplendent in a smart school uniform, would find the school buildings clustered beyond the gateway. What a contrast and welcome relief these were from the dark Victorian buildings that had been endured for over six years of infant and primary schooling; the covered passageways, heated cloakrooms and light airy classrooms of Redworth provided a perfect learning environment. The school was custom-built in 1938 as part of the county authority's plan for reorganisation of rural schools, so that they were clearly divided into separate senior and junior institutions. After the 1944 Education Act, which introduced the concept of secondary education for all pupils, the school became Redworth Secondary Modern and the following year Redworth County Secondary Modern.

In September 1960, many of us trekked from Smithfields to Redworth for our first day of secondary modern schooling. We gathered in the seemingly large Assembly Hall to be sorted into classes, these being categorised A, B, or C according to alphabetical order. It felt a little like sheep being divided up at market as each group trailed after its appointed teacher 'like lambs to the slaughter'! There was a form teacher for each class and mine, through the years at the school, were Mr Owen (1B), Mr Murch (2B), Mr Molland (3B) and Mr Voss (4B), whilst our 5th year 'O' level group was registered by Mr Martin.

Other teachers recalled include Mr Barter, who taught history, Mr Parker responsible for geography, Mr Blight who attempted to inspire us with poetry lessons, Miss Wilson for English and literature and John Crout, whose subjects included maths and technical drawing. John Maries taught art, but was also a good cricketer; on sunny summer mornings we would forsake the art room for a spot of welcome cricket practice.

It was a new experience to have English and maths, supplemented by specific science lessons. To be entrusted with chemicals, taken from cabinets full of interesting substances that lined the laboratory, was a whole new experience. It was also something of a novelty to sit on such high stools. There were also the flaming Bunsen burners, which produced interesting results when we heated certain materials, and much enjoyment was found in the properties of quicksilver or mercury. It fell to Mr 'Nobby' Clarke to perform the unenviable task of organising our science lessons. Miss Knapman was an excellent maths teacher who had such favourite expressions, or outpourings of emotion, as "Angels and ministers of grace defend us!" when our answers to mathematical equations were well off the mark.

There was an amusing moment when we had turned up in Class One, where she took maths lessons, and one of the boys climbed behind the sliding blackboard, which doubled as a sort of storage space. Another pupil slid the blackboard into place leaving him completely hidden from sight. Just at that crucial moment, Miss Knapman arrived and conducted the whole lesson whilst the poor lad remained silently entombed behind a board full of quadratic equations!

Being new arrivals at the school, we had a visit from the Gideon Society and every pupil was presented with a bible.

All secondary modern schools had woodwork rooms. The one at Redworth was the domain of Mr Richardson, who instructed us on the art of basic carpentry to produce such useful items as stools and stands. Meanwhile, the girls, in an age of apparent inequality, were instructed in the skills of needlework and domestic science.

The school had a well-stocked library and here Mr Voss, who incidentally bowled excellent off spinners on the leg side, often took classes. His wife also taught at the school. The shelves were stacked with a surprising range of reading material. There was a wonderful selection of old almanacs and also classics such as Masefield's *Jim Davis*, the novels of Charles Dickens and the poems of Walter de la Mare. However, during the regular reading sessions, I enjoyed reading up on the results of past cricket test matches!

Beyond the immediate school buildings was the gardening hut, which, as its name suggests, was for rural science lessons. Nearby were the school gardens; the theory would be conducted in the hut whilst we were 'let loose' on the practical side of the subject in those garden plots accessed through the potting shed.

There was an alternative, unofficial and more 'picturesque' way of getting to school, which possibly shortened the daily walk for some, especially if late. This was reached from the top of Barracks Hill and took one through the gardens and onto the paths beside the playing fields. On this green sward football, rugby and hockey were played; there were netball and tennis courts that were overlooked by the windows of the classrooms, offering a welcome distraction from lessons. Competitions included the Webber's Shield Knock-Out and the Blessington Cup for soccer, whilst runners had the opportunity to compete in the area cross-country and athletics competitions.

Redworth boasted a fully equipped gym, which included such delights as wall-bars, horses, ropes and a selection of apparatus including the weighty medicine ball. There was also the luxury of showers! Les Downes was the master in charge of games and a keen cricketer who played for the Totnes club; he encouraged some of us to go on and play for the town. Others went on to play rugby or football on the town park.

The games mistress at that time was Mrs Strutt. When it came to inter-class rivalry, we tended to lose out in competitions, classes A and C having the sporting prowess, but this was somewhat rectified by the division of the whole school into four houses, namely Drake, Raleigh, Frobisher and Grenville. Although having the unenviable record of three no throws in the javelin, I was cricket house captain of Raleigh and managed to gain my school colours.

Redworth also sought to serve the community; small groups of pupils would visit hospitals and old people's homes, in addition to supporting the Red Cross and charities for the visually impaired.

Other outdoor activities included youth hostelling and a residential week at Prince Hall, near Two Bridges on Dartmoor, as well as the trips for the Devon and Dartmoor Society.

Mr Rundle was an excellent Headmaster, and his strong leadership provided a revolutionary step in making it possible for more able students to take GCE 'O' levels. This was achieved through established links with the Girls' High School, where the available teaching skills and expertise enabled pupils to experience more advanced studies. I must have been one of the few to be educated at Redworth, the Girls' High School and later at the old Grammar School Mansion!

I well remember the night before those first 'O' levels, lying awake unable to get to sleep, whilst outside in the gardens of the estate the neighbours were busy tilling their ground; the steady click of spade on turf continued until darkness. It was then that my dear mother, who was going into hospital the following day, came in to talk with me.

Sadly, the final Redworth Speech Day occurred on 2 December 1965. The *Totnes Times*, with a centre-page spread, gave a comprehensive report of the occasion. Dr Elmhirst presided as Chairman and Mr Crawford, former HM Inspector of Schools, gave an address and presented the prizes. The proceedings finished with the National Anthem, thus concluding another chapter in the history of education in Totnes and ushering in the new era of the Comprehensive system.

Church and Chapel

On first coming to Totnes, my mother greatly felt the need to go to church and she recorded in her diary, "The very first Sunday in Totnes, I faithfully kept my promise to God and went along to Church." In conversation with Mrs Winchester, she found out that there was a St John's Church just across the bridge in Bridgetown. This was wonderful, because that was the name of the church she had attended back in Nelson.

Mother then began to attend the services at St Mary's and here also worked with the children in the Sunday School; at one stage she was responsible for speaking at the curate's Bible class for teenage boys.

Sometime after this she became a committed Christian. At the time of this dramatic experience she was working at Tucker's Sweet Factory; shortly afterwards, she moved to Hayman's, drapers, outfitters and furnishers in High Street.

She also changed her place of worship to the Totnes Gospel Hall, a chapel in Castle Street that was erected in 1924. On Sunday afternoons, she would collect a large number of children from the district and take them to Sunday School there. After the Second World War, my father, along with

his mother, also went to the Gospel Hall, and we would attend their meetings as a family. I remember sitting with Granny during evening services and afterwards walking home with her through the Narrows and down Collins Road to The Little Shrubbery to sample her wonderful home-made jam sponge!

From an early age we went to Sunday School, which started at 3 p.m. The whole of the Sunday School stayed together for the first half of the hour-long meeting, conducted by the superintendent. We would sing choruses such as 'Wide, wide as the ocean', 'Climb, climb up sunshine mountain' and 'Echo, echo,

echo'. Most of the choruses were accompanied by actions, 'Jesus loves me – this I know' being a classic example where the juvenile congregation would become kangaroos, Eskimos or Indians when the appropriate word was sung.

When the Sunday School broke up into groups, individual teachers would have Bible readings with talks and quizzes; the infants sometimes were given colouring tasks. Sometimes there would be visiting speakers, each with their individual brand of presentation, or nightly children's campaigns over the period of a week. There would be the added incentive of visual aids or flannelgraphs with stickers for attendance, sweets for correct answers and prizes for memorising biblical texts.

At one time we were invited to the Tin-tab at Bridgetown; this was a corrugated construction of very basic design.

Monday evenings during term-time were given over to children's meetings and these started at six o'clock; at that time, as the allure of television was not great, the numbers attending often reached 60.

Late January was the time when the Annual Prize Giving took place and this was held on a Saturday evening. The main hall would be festooned with balloons and decorations, with a huge Christmas tree laden with prizes placed in the corner.

First, the teachers had their tea in an upstairs room, along with specially invited guests. Later on the children would have food brought around to them, which would be eaten whilst they sat in their seats (no tables). There were inevitable spillages over party clothes.

After the meal, recitations were on 'the menu' for the evening's events. Groups or individuals performed for the pleasure of the watching adults, but this proved to be something of an ordeal for many of the nervous participants. However, this was somewhat compensated for when the prizes for attendance were distributed. For my reward, I managed to collect the *Jungle Doctor* stories by Paul White and, later on, an excellent series of books, on which he collaborated with David Britten,

called the Ranford Series. These were set in Australia.

This photograph shows the Totnes Gospel Hall Girls' Sewing Class party in 1962. Featured are Mrs Santer, Miss Eileen Fisher (Iles), Miss Taylor, Mrs Back, Mrs Wyse and Mr Back. This was a group which was originated many years earlier by Miss Taylor and my mother, Doris Chapman.

At that time the Tarring family, who owned the bakery in the Narrows, attended the Chapel. Father oversaw the business; Mother handled cash and book-keeping; one son, Claude, controlled the bakehouse; while the other son, Edward, went on deliveries. The business was only a few yards from the Hall and wooden trays laden with tuffs, currant buns, cakes and loaves of bread were easily carried across to Castle Street. The Tarrings also had two daughters: Muriel, who was responsible for the youngest pupils in the Sunday School, and Kathleen.

The Sunday School Treat

From the ice, snow and wet of those dark January nights we looked forward to the long summer days, which included 'The Outing'. My diary for 25 June 1959 notes: "We are going to Teignmouth today and Dad gave me two shillings and sixpence to spend." I remember the feeling of excitement and exhilaration the night before as we were weeding the front garden; from time to time a train would puff by at the bottom of the road, conjuring up thoughts of that journey in a packed railway carriage on its way to golden sands.

Families such as the Sansoms, Denleys, Backs, Taylors, Santers, Winters, Whitells, Bromings, Tarrings, Lears and Sparkes were members of the meeting in the 1950s.

Everyone would muster at the Hall in readiness for the 'treat', as it was called.

A prayer, chorus and Bible reading from the superintendent took place, before a chattering crocodile of girls wearing summer dresses and lads sporting open-necked shirts could be seen wending its way down Castle Hill, carrying buckets, spades, baskets and hampers – all the trappings for a great day out.

For a number of years, the Methodists also joined our group for the event.

The railway company provided additional coaches for the journey. The platform would be filled with children and adults, who had been supplied with special tickets for both the rail journey and the tea, so that there was no last-minute panic at the booking office when the 9.50 scheduled special train arrived.

At Teignmouth, families and groups 'pitched camp' on the sand; there must be many an old photograph, now gathering dust, of deck-chairs, knotted hankies for headgear, children building sandcastles, or figures paddling at the water's edge.

During the afternoon most would gather on the 'green' (usually a dirty 'brown' by this time of summer) known as The Den, across the road, where games and sports were held. Packets of sweets were given to the winners.

After a tea of cakes, jam tuffs, sandwiches and sausage rolls (courtesy of Tarring's) the return journey would take place on the 6.45 p.m. from Teignmouth. Usually there would be an engine parked in the loop line for us to observe, before an assembly of rather weary and sunburnt people, many with sticky mouths and hands from the tea or the candy floss, climbed into the welcome refuge of a waiting carriage before departing for Totnes.

'Abide with Me'

For me, in later years, there were the Bible Class and the Friday Youth Club, with a coffee bar where we would listen to records such as 'This World is not my Home' and 'Down by the Riverside'. Groups would attend summer camps at Mortehoe, near Woolacombe in North Devon. There were also the Easter house parties, which were great fun. This photograph shows our group at the Maranatha Hotel in Ilfracombe in 1966.

Meetings were attended by those from all social backgrounds; intelligence, social standing, age and nationality are of no significance in the eyes of God! Our groups of young people would take part in gospel meetings, singing and speaking in various places. Memories of certain hymns still remain, such as 'Abide with me' and 'Just as I am', as well as the verse John 3:16: *"For God so loved the world, that he gave his only begotten Son, that whosoever believeth in him should not perish, but have everlasting life."*

Totnes Carnival

Each year the Carnival would take place as one of the important events of the calendar. As with the Coronation procession, the initial gathering was in the streets of Smithfields and adjoining Collapark. There was always an array of floats, as well as of those who formed up to be a part of the walking section of the parade.

There were the regular contributions made by organisations such as the local Fire Brigade and Totnes Band (of which my sister, Anne, was a member).

Most of these accompanying photos were taken in the late 1960s and early 1970s.

No carnival was complete without the Carnival Queen; these photographs show the crowning ceremony of Miss Totnes with her Ladies-in-Waiting and scenes of other 'Queens'. The interesting scene in North Street below these is of the St Mary's Girls' Club carnival float of 1954.

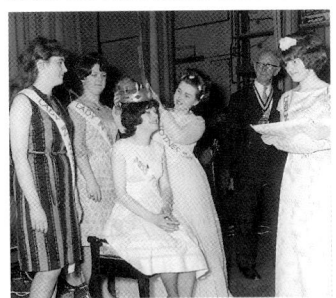

The Totnes Show

Held beside the road to Berry Pomeroy, another annual event, the Totnes Show, has, since its inception at the beginning of the last century, continued through the years as an attraction for visitors and local people. Written many years ago, the *Western Morning News* set the scene: "*It is truly said of the Totnes and District Show that it has something for everybody to do and see. Continuing to make greater appeal to farmers, townspeople and holidaymakers year after year, the one day competitive show of farm stock, horses, sheep, pigs, dogs, flowers, vegetables and handicrafts is backed with pageantry and entertainment in which hundreds of performers will take part.*" The event remains largely the same.

Touring Fairs

These were also an eagerly awaited source of entertainment; during our schooldays they would set up on waste ground. The attractions included Bumper Cars, the Big Wheel, coconut shies and many sideshows and stalls, along with kiosks selling the traditional 'fayre' of such events – toffee apples and candy floss.

A Whale of a Time?

Our next-door neighbours were Mr and Mrs Rayner; their daughter, Joy, would often take me out to places like the park. I recall there was once a rather unusual attraction – a travelling whale that could be viewed on the back of a trailer.

My diary entry for 23 May 1959 states: "I went to Billy Smart's Circus at Goodrington today with Glenda. There were 22 acts. We travelled around Berry Pomeroy to get there." My friend Glenda Viney lived in Smithfields with her parents, at a point along the top Plymouth Road.

Door to Door

In those days many items were either delivered to or collected from your door. Numerous people derived a living from handling daily wares. The coalman visited most houses, because people had coal fires. There were few people who owned a washing machine, so it was a common practice for the weekly wash to be collected and, some time later, delivered back to households. Everybody got their milk from roundsmen; in our case it was Margaret Wellington, of Hooper's Dairy, who supplied us on a daily basis for many years. The baker also called; for us it was a man who worked for Hill, Palmer and Edwards. Then there was the weekly 'Pop' lorry that carried Corona drinks in bottles with spring tops – our favourite was Dandelion and Burdock. Other regular callers included the fruit and veg man.

A Good Read?

Our newsagent was Cummings in the High Street. The daily paper regularly landed through the letterbox before school and, in the 1950s, was often accompanied by magazines such as *Enid Blyton's Magazine* and *Sunny Stories*. About a decade later, I looked forward to receiving the *Boys' Own Paper* and *Meccano Magazine*. My sister would receive her comics, namely *Playhour* and *Harold Hare*, followed later by *Princess*.

A Good Listen?

The wireless in our sitting room provided us with series such as *Jennings Goes to School* (by Anthony Buckeridge), *Clara Chuff and her Friends*, *The Clitheroe Kid* and *Norman and Henry Bones*. It required an accumulator, a battery which had to be taken into Stoyle's the electricians, who were located in the Narrows, for recharging.

Pocket Money

During the long school summer holidays, it was important to earn some pocket money, so in 1964 I started on the morning shift at Dawe's Creamery. Armed with a National Insurance card and clocking in at 7.30 a.m., I went to work amongst the milk cartons and 'Golden Bloom' orange juice containers, my menial job being to place crates of empty bottles onto a conveyor belt ready for washing. However, things later improved. Thanks to my father being in the dairy trade, a more interesting holiday job at the creamery involved working in the cream room under Bob Uden.

Bob, whose son Don later played cricket for Totnes, would later take us over the fields to practise batting and bowling on a pitch of 'uneven bounce'. This had often been 'roughed up' by the cows that were fielding at various unorthodox positions, 'deep mid-cowpat' and so on, whilst we held our unofficial matches!

As a result of these labours at the creamery, I purchased a Westminster transistor radio from Currys, next to the Midland Bank in High Street. This provided the latest pop music of the day from acts such as the Beatles, the Searchers, Peter and Gordon, Gerry and the Pacemakers, The Bachelors, The Seekers, Cilla Black, The Tremeloes and many others. Thursday was *Top of the Pops* on the television, and the week's number one record was eagerly awaited. Records could be bought at Pinch's, the electricians retail store, which was next to Frisby's shoe shop.

Along with the creamery, the major employers in Totnes during the 1950s and 1960s were

Harris's Bacon Factory (the site now of Safeway's supermarket), Reeves the timber merchants, beside the Dart, and Tucker's sweet factory, all now consigned to the memory.

Meanwhile, I gained further work experience at Evans and Cutler, whose garage stood in North Street. Here I was engaged as an apprentice mechanic and my tasks included minor repairs, working the petrol pump and trekking up past Crawford's shop to Tarring's with the all-important task of collecting 'bun' orders. Here, overlooked by the Castle, one was

reminded of schooldays, when we would play in this area. Access was gained by way of climbing the bank from Malt Mill (we called it Moat Mill), traipsing across the fields, shinnying over the low wall and into the grounds.

There was also access via the North Gate arch and this gave the opportunity to play in the surrounding area, where, as this photograph shows, an old German field gun once stood (it was used as scrap metal for the war effort).

Local children also liked to participate in the Beating of the Bounds, as seen here in 1969 with a sprightly Bill Bennett stepping it out in the middle of a large group.

For generations Totnesians (and visitors) have struggled up the steep route from The Plains, which takes them from Fore Street into High Street and through the Narrows to the top Plymouth Road. Loaded shopping bags, carriers, briefcases, pushchairs, prams, bicycles and carts have all been used to transport goods to and from shops and businesses along this route.

The Borough Park

Mention has already been made of the importance of the Borough Park as a centre for events and celebrations. It has also been a valuable daily and weekly resource for games and recreation, providing a home venue for team sports such as rugby, football and cricket. The accompanying

photographs give an idea some of the players who graced this sporting arena over the years.

To gain the best all-round view of the Park, as it looked in the 1950s and 1960s, we might well, in our mind's eye, walk out to bat for Totnes Cricket Club on a summer's day. After taking guard, we see the opposition's fast bowler come tearing towards us, and a fraction of a second later the ball fizzes past the edge of the bat and has thudded into the wicket-keeper's gloves. Being the last ball of the over there is time to look around and take in the scene …

The Pavilion is dotted with white-flannelled figures in various stages of preparation for batting; surrounding this activity the Park gardens are ablaze with colour, whilst to the right of the Pavilion come sounds of activity from the bowling green. Behind this stretch are the tennis courts and the sound of ball upon racket. To the left of the scene lie the roundabout, slide, horse and swings of the children's play area, and beyond, in the distance, the rockery beside one of the entrances. These tended to be at the four extremities of the Park, with another half-way along Station Road. Behind

the point where we are standing once lay the Church School gardens with a little hut. When it rained the whole group would rush to attempt to squash into the confined space. Beyond the distant entrance was the Drill Hall.

A necessary resource was the park tap, which provided water for thirsty (and perspiring) young sportsmen and women.

A clink of ball on bat announces the gradual accumulation of runs or the sporadic fall of wickets; distant sounds from Dawe's Creamery, the railway station and a transistor radio are audible, as members of the batting team listen to England's progress in the current test match.

Teabreak arrives with a choice of sandwiches and cakes, the warm sun allowing the players the luxury of sitting or lying on the grass before a final session in the field up to the 7.30 'stumps' call. All around are neatly cut grass and carefully tended flowerbeds, whilst 'yonder' lies the heavy roller in readiness for action.

Evening shadows of trees, buildings and the players in the middle start to lengthen across the park. A golden glow reveals a fast-sinking sun as deck-chairs are folded away, heralding the close of play and of another day in the life of the Borough Park.

A Peep into 1970s Totnes

The new era of the 1970s saw changes afoot for me, and also for the town of Totnes.

On a very wet Tuesday afternoon in late September, I was a passenger in a car driven by my friend Dave Back. I was on my way to St Luke's College, Exeter, the foremost PE training establishment for teachers (along with Loughborough), to spend three years training to be a teacher.

The beginning of the decade saw the institution of Elizabethan Day, which occurred on Tuesdays and turned the quietest trading day into the busiest. Local shopkeepers dressed in Elizabethan costumes and the special market has become a regular weekly event, with a variety of stalls and activities, through the summer season.

The 1970s changing landscape of Totnes witnessed the end of the historic Almshouses; parts of these could be traced back some 400 years, but, classed as unfit for habitation, the Borough Council subsequently placed a demolition order upon them. They had been built in 1600 on The Plains; in 1830, parts of the buildings deemed suitable were moved to their final site in the Grove, which was then a waste spot called the Carrion Pits.

Our final picture is a reminder of the importance of our local services and the vital role that they

play in the community; it features the firemen of Totnes in the 1970s.

It is an interesting experience to visit past times by word and picture, to make comparisons with our present-day situation and lifestyle, and to realise that change can be positive and profitable. Sometimes, it is comforting to turn back the clock to relive those sights and sounds of yesteryear that evoke so many memories.